Shaw in Love

The Private Life
of George Bernard Shaw

Elizabeth Sharland

iUniverse, Inc.
Bloomington

The Private Life of George Bernard Shaw
Shaw in Love

iUniverse books may be ordered through booksellers or by contacting:

iUniverse
1663 Liberty Drive
Bloomington, IN 47403
www.iuniverse.com
1-800-Authors (1-800-288-4677)

Because of the dynamic nature of the Internet, any web addresses or links contained in this book may have changed since publication and may no longer be valid. The views expressed in this work are solely those of the author and do not necessarily reflect the views of the publisher, and the publisher hereby disclaims any responsibility for them.

Any people depicted in stock imagery provided by Thinkstock are models, and such images are being used for illustrative purposes only.

Certain stock imagery © Thinkstock.

ISBN: 978-1-4620-2421-6 (sc)
ISBN: 978-1-4620-2422-3 (ebook)

Printed in the United States of America

iUniverse rev. date: 7/13/2011

THIS PLAY IS DEDICATED TO THE LATE BARRY MORSE

Barry Morse first directed and produced the play for the Theatre Museum London, and subsequently for the Performing Arts Lodge in Toronto, Canada. Barry played GBS.

Also performed at the Algonquin Hotel in New York with Michael Allison, Rosemary Harris, Carol Higgins Clark and Barrie Ingham.

George Bernard Shaw

INTRODUCTION

Anyone who has ever read or seen a play by George Bernard Shaw is usually curious to read more about the man. His works are still as popular today and they were in his day, although perhaps he is not talked about quite so much at present. Every few years another writer publishes another biography about him and he must be one of England's best known playwrights, up there with Shakespeare. Ever since I acted in St. Joan years ago and had memories of other great actresses who had played her, from Sybil Thorndike to Imogen Stubbs. Any actor who plays a lead in a Shaw play remembers the effect of one of his plays has on an audience.

St. Joan is a marvelous part, but then so are many others women's roles, including Lisa in Pygmalion, originated by Wendy Hiller.

Barry Morse, the late President of the prestigious Shaw Society in England probably knew more about his life than anyone, except perhaps Michael Holroyd, who wrote a four volume biography several years ago. When I wrote the book 'The British on Broadway' Barry kindly wrote the Foreword to the book, as he was a theatre historian as well as a Broadway and West End actor. I am including his contribution here because it describes Shaw and his American stay.

I passionately wanted to see where Shaw lived. Because everyone wrote what a simple and almost monastic life he lead at Ayot. He was a vegetarian, and also a non-drinker, who believed in physical exercise and no doubt, cold baths and no central heating. He and his wife Charlotte, who he married late in life, lived there until the end of their lives. It is a well known fact, that their marriage was not consummated and that Charlotte was more of a helpmate, companion and secretary.

He had a small wooden hut made in the garden, where he could work in private without distractions from the house, although he did have a telephone extension put in, to be used only in emergencies. He had the hut built so that it could be turned slowly to follow the sun, whenever there was sun, as he was working. This little hut is still there, and his desk and chair and small day bed. I was fascinated to stand there, at the door of the hut, alone, the only sound was the sound of the birds in the nearby tree, and imagine how many hours, days, years he wrote inside this tiny space. I imagined him being there, and I wanted to talk to him although I think he would have told me to bugger off.

The day I visited the house and grounds, I was the only visitor so I was granted some privileges. I was allowed to play his small upright piano, and to sit down in his living room which still contained many of his books and furniture. The dining room was sparse and very cold. I couldn't imagine the two of them, seated there without heat, meat or wine!

The kitchen was just as cold and severe. It must have been extremely bitter in the winter months. The exterior of the red brick house is really quite ugly, and gives the impression of a school house almost, with very small windows and not much of a view.

The gardens are better, especially in the back of the house. There is a large lawn and flower beds beyond as well as a fair number of trees.

Many of his guests who visited him there wrote how well he looked but how difficult it was to find the house.

He also kept a flat in London and would drive up to Ayot each weekend. Years later he gave up his London hope and remained in the country.

Each year, around the anniversary of his birthday, there is a mini Shaw Festival with a company of actors presenting one or two of his short plays in the garden at the back of the house. The actors using the doors of the house for the entrances and exits, and one suddenly imagines that Shaw himself, might come through one of the doors to take a bow after the play ends. It is a charming Festival. People bring their own baskets of food, and picnic on the lawn facing the back of the house, either bringing their own little tables, or eating on the grass. Bottles of wine appear, and as the sunsets on a summer evening, the place becomes quite magical. Every year the Shaw Society fosters new talent and the actors love the environment and the inspiration of acting in the playwright's garden.

Shaw was amazingly prolific. Not only did he write plays, books and articles, there was a massive output of correspondence, he used to write to hundreds of people, so you wonder when he found the time to entertain at all.

He loved writing to actresses who were playing in his plays. He fell in love with at least two of them, Ellen Terry and Mrs. Patrick Campbell, or "Stella" as he nicknamed her.

Barry Morse produced the play at the Theatre Museum in London with eleven women, he played GBS in his Norfolk jacket and Irish accent. We also did a reading at the Algonquin Hotel in New York, with Barrie Ingham playing Shaw and Rosemary Harris, Carol Higgins-Clark and Arlene Stern. The play explains the dilemma Shaw had about meeting Ellen Terry. He wrote to her almost every day but never met her. One evening she looked through the peephole in the curtain on stage and caught a glimpse of him.

He was also writing almost every day to Mrs. Patrick Campbell and his letters to her are still in print.

He lived at that time with his mother in Tavistock Square, but they rarely ate together or saw each other even though they were in the same house. He was racing from one political meeting, to another, and neglecting himself and his health. His foot became infected and he didn't bother to bandage it properly so it got worse. He needed a secretary and began wondering if he was going to survive the workload and his health.

Charlotte Payne Townsend was suggested as a secretary through friends, and when she came for an interview she was appalled. She described his room as completely chaotic. There were heaps of letters, pages of manuscripts, books, knives, forks spoons, sometimes a cup of cocoa or a half finished plate of porridge, a saucepan, and a dozen other things were mixed up indiscriminately and all undusted, as he said that his papers must not be touched. "I knew something had to be done."

Later on after she had got to know him, she realized that his mother couldn't take care of him or herself, she offered to find a place in the country and take care of him but not without marriage.

He was too ill to go out and get a ring and a license, but asked her to do so. He then wrote that he found that his own objection to marriage had ceased with his objection to his own death. Charlotte settled an annuity on his mother, as she couldn't afford to keep herself. She had become rather neurotic and had taken to ouija boards and séances and had ideas on the unseen forces beyond the material world. So the couple were married in Henrietta Street in Covent Garden. Shaw wrote "We were married on June 1ˢᵗ in a registry office. It was pouring with rain. Of the two witnesses we had, Sydney Olivier, who was much better dressed than I, was mistaken for the groom and because of my rather shabby attire, I was thought of as someone off the street who'd been called in as a witness. This prompted Charlotte to buy me new clothes. I was a married man at last."

Shortly after they moved into the country house, Shaw who was using crutches, fell down the staircase and broke his foot, which meant more time on crutches and time in bed.

Charlotte wrote that she was only ever jealous of Stella Campbell. Much of his philandering filled him with shame and disgust, but it did not cure him. It came easily and naturally to him, as to many Irishmen and it readily and irresistibly appealed to English women unaccustomed to Irish Blarney. He said he was surprised when English women took his flatteries and courtesies and endearments for serious intentions instead of light hearted attentions as he meant them to be. So, often he had to hastily reverse his engines.

However he learned to put his philandering to severely practical uses and to employ it as a means of obtaining, first, the interest, then the goodwill, and finally the cooperation and services of famous actresses. He succeeded. What he was trying to do was both human and natural. Shaw wrote that he thought marriage is an acquired taste, like "olives or eating winkles with a pin' and thought perhaps that he ought never to have been married.

He wrote that some of his most gratifying relationships with women were on paper. "Let those who complain that it was all on paper know that only on paper has humanity achieved truth, beauty, virtue and abiding love."

His sister Lucy often visited, but she thought he was rather weird. Saying that he won't eat meat and now he won't touch alcohol. He is quite determined to forego roast lamb for vegetables. "He will become a head full of brains and underneath he will be all woolly underwear and vegetables."

Two of the passions of George Bernard Shaw - apart from his women who he preferred to keep between the sheets, paper that is, not bed sheets - were undoubtedly music and religion.

One of the earliest musical influences on the young Shaw was a man named George John Lee, a music teacher and organizer of concerts, who taught Shaw's mother then became associated with her and eventually lived with the family in Dublin and later London. Lee moved in with the family when Shaw was seven. Detesting her husband, who she called a failure and a drunkard, Lee became her new center of gravity. According to Shaw, who wrote about him much later in life, Lee was a man of "mesmeric vitality and force." As a teacher of singing, Lee claimed he could make his young lady students sing 'like Patti" (a famous diva of the time) in twelve lessons at a guinea a lesson.

The introduction of Lee into the Shaw household dramatically increased the young man's interest in music. It was through Lee that music became a dominating influence in his life. By the time he was a teenager he could sing and whistle from end to end leading works by Handel, Haydn, Mozart, Beethoven, Rossini and Verdi.

When the Shaw family, minus the father George Carr Shaw, moved with Lee to London, George junior was 17. He stayed with his father in Dublin for three years then he moved to London himself to live with his mother, his two sisters and Lee, who had renamed himself Vandeleur Lee. The London that the shy, beardless youth arrived in in1876 was very much the gaslit city of Sherlock Holmes. Charles Dickens had only been dead five years. In the year the young man came to London, Edison was contemplating the idea of recording sound on a revolving cylinder, and twelve months later the phonograph became a reality. Two years later electric light was established and the age of gaslight was over.

Shaw first started writing about music by ghost writing articles for Lee for a publication called The Hornet. His criticisms were so severe Lee, (under whose name the reviews appeared) was fired.

His next journalistic endeavors in music writing came when a tall, restrained Scot of his own age, William Archer, obtained work for Shaw as music critic for The Dramatic Review and the Magazine of Music. Meanwhile, he was writing his youthful, and not very successful novels, one of them being "Love Among the Artists" the hero of which is a

British Beethoven, named Owen Jack, who Shaw described as utterly unreasonable and unaccountable "but a vital genius, powerful in an art that is beyond logic and even beyond words."

Some years later Shaw was able to write, "I could make deaf stockbrokers read my two pages on music … the alleged joke being that I knew nothing about it. The real joke was that I knew all about it."

In 1888, when Shaw was thirty-two, T. P. O'Connor founded The Star and invited Shaw, who was now a Socialist, to join the political staff of his new paper. When he read Shaw's first article he told him that it would be 500 years before such radical stuff could be acceptable as political journalism. But, unwilling to sack a fellow Irishmen, the new editor offered him a column on music, but with the stipulation that he not write anything about Bach in B Minor. Typically, Shaw's first review began, "The number of empty seats at the performance of Bach's Mass in B Minor at St James's Hall on Saturday did little credit to the artistic culture of which the West End is supposed to be the universal center …"

He wrote for The Star under the pseudonym Corno di Bassetto, meaning a basset horn. Soon after joining The Star Shaw was summoned to the editor's office. "The fact is, my dear Corno," Shaw recalled he said, "I don't believe that music in London is confined to St James's Hall, Covent Garden and the Albert Hall. People must sing and play elsewhere …" So, in his next review, Shaw wrote, "A little later the train was rushing through the strangest places: Shoreditch, of which I had read in historical novels; Old Ford, which I had supposed to be a character in one of Shakespeare's plays; Homerton, which is associated in my mind with pigeons; and Haggerston, a name perfectly new to me. When I got into the concert room I was perfectly dazzled by the appearance of the orchestra. Nearly all the desks for the second violins were occupied by ladies: beautiful young ladies. Personal beauty is not a strong point of West End orchestras, and I thought the change an immense improvement until the performance began, when the fair fiddlers rambled from bar to bar with a sweet indecision that had a charm of its own, but was not exactly what Purcell and Handel meant." He ends his review with the comment, "I am, on the whole, surprised and delighted with the East End, and shall soon venture there without my revolver."

Shaw's approach to religion also had an irreverent edge to it. Perhaps this started with his father who, despite being a self-effacing nonentity, bequeathed his son the sense of anti-climactic humor. Shaw recalls, "When I scoffed at the Bible, my father quite sincerely rebuke me, telling me with what little sternness was in his nature, that I should not speak so; that no educated man would make such a display of ignorance; that the Bible was universally recognized as a literary and historical masterpiece; and as much more to the same effect as he could muster. But when he had reached the point of feeling really impressive, a convulsion of internal chuckling would wrinkle up his eyes; and (I knowing all the time what was coming) would cap his eulogy by assuring me, with an air of perfect fairness, that even the worst enemy of religion could say no worse of the Bible than that it was the damndest parcel of lies ever written." Shaw also recalls how they were once visited by a Unitarian. When he asked his father what a Unitarian was George Carr Shaw explained that a Unitarian was one who did not believe that Jesus was crucified, in that he was observed running down the far side of the hill of Calvary.

There is a lot of humor but also deep intellectual curiosity in Shaw's writing about religion. He wrote five plays that he considered religious: Back to Methuselah, Androcles and the Lion, Saint Joan (for which he won the Nobel Prize and which many people consider his best play), The Simpleton of the Unexpected Isles and The Adventures of the Black Girl in her search for God. The latter, in which he has this young lady meeting all sorts of people who say they are God, got him into a lot of trouble with a very dear friend, Dame Laurentia McLachlan, a Benedictine nun who became the Abbess of Stanbrook Abbey in England.

Writing to her in a discussion about St. Joan, he wrote, "My dear Sister Laurentia, in reading heathen literature like mine, you must remember that I am addressing an audience not exclusively Catholic, it included not only Protestants but also Indians and Orientals. If I wrote from an exclusively Catholic point of view my book would reach no further than the penny lives of the saints which they sell in the Churches of Ireland. I want my sound to go out into all lands!"

But he went too far when he sent her his new book, the Black Girl. Dame McLachlan wrote to him, "If you had written against my father or my mother, you would not expect to be forgiven or received until you had made amends. I implore you to suppress this book and retract its blasphemies." Shaw wrote back to her in protest but, she did not reply.

Over a year later he received through the post a small buff-colored card with the inscription "In Memory of September 6th, 1884 - 1934. Dame Laurentia McLachlan, Abbess of Stanbrook."

Shaw penned the following. "To the Ladies of Stanbrook Abbey, Worcester. Dear Sisters, I have just received the news of the death of Dame Laurentia McLachlan. I had no knowledge of the state of her health and no suspicion that I should never see her again on this earth. There was a time when I was in such grace with her that she asked you all to pray for me; and I valued your prayers most sincerely. I wrote a little book which, to my grief, shocked Dame Laurentia so much that I dare not show my face at the Abbey until I was forgiven. She has, I am sure, forgiven me now; but I wish she could tell me so. In the outside world, from which you have escaped, it is sometimes necessary to shock people violently to make them think seriously about religion; and my ways were too rough. I have no right to your prayers; but if I should occasionally be remembered by those of you who recall my old visits I should be none the worse for them, and very grateful. Yours faithfully, G. Bernard Shaw.

In a strange, ironic twist, the small buff-colored card was not to commemorate Dame McLachlan's death but merely a souvenir of her Golden Jubilee in the Benedictine habit. But it broke their silence and they remained friends for years to come.

Earlier in their friendship Shaw announced that he was to become a pilgrim in fact. He announced to her that he was going to visit Jerusalem. Dame Laurentia girlishly asked him to bring back a little memento from Calvary. At the conclusion of his trip, Shaw wrote: "You asked me for a relic from Calvary – but Calvary is only a spot on the church pavement, jealously guarded, and with nothing removable about it. Where the real Calvary is nobody knows; for the hills outside the city are innumerable. The alleged Via Dolorosa I traversed in a motor car hooting furiously at the children to get out of my way. So off I went to Bethlehem; and from the threshold of the Church of the Nativity, I picked up a little stone, a scrap of limestone rock that certainly existed when the feet of Jesus pattered about on it and the feet of Mary pursued him to keep him in order. In fact I picked up two little stones: one to be thrown blindfold among the others in Stanbrook garden so that there may always be a stone from Bethlehem there, and nobody will know which it is and be tempted to steal it, and the other for your own self."

A mutual friend of both of them, Sir Sydney Cockerell, Director of the Fitzwilliam Museum in Cambridge, observed that there was no inscription on the reliquary containing the stones. He asked, "Wouldn't it be a good idea to put a brief inscription explaining its purpose and saying who it's from?"

Shaw replied: "Cockerell is a heathen atheist: a reliquary is no more to him than a football cup. What the devil – saving your cloth – could we put on it? We couldn't put our names on it – could we? That seems to me perfectly awful. 'An inscription explaining its purpose!' If we could explain its purpose we could explain the universe. I couldn't. Could you? If Cockerell thinks he can – and he's quite capable of it – let him try, and submit the result to the Pope. Dear Sister: our fingerprints are on the stone, and Heaven knows whose footprints may be on it. Isn't that enough?"

The British Production

When this play was to be performed at London's Theatre Museum, my father, Barry Morse, asked me to cast the womens' roles from among actors I had worked with. I was lucky enough to obtain the consent of eight first rate performers. Among them was a lady who had worked in British regional theatre with Barry before I was born and then later with me in provincial productions in The U.K.. After many years she was again acting with her old friend Barry and I found that very touching. All the women I had suggested gave excellent performances in this fine play, which was received with tremendous enthusiasm by the packed house, and I was pleased to have been a small contributor to it's success.

As a footnote to the Private Life of Bernard Shaw, many people may think of G.B.S. as having had little or no sexual experience whereas, in truth, he was seduced by an older woman (an unmarried friend of his mother's) when he was 29 and had affairs with other single women before his marriage to Charlotte. It was then that he proclaimed to the world that theirs was to be a celibate union. This, I think, was largely taken to be an aesthetic choice on his part. In fact, it was Charlotte's stipulation, on accepting his proposal, that the marriage should not be consummated and despite his many chaste infatuations with, among others, Mrs. Patrick Campbell and Ellen Terry, it was a long and deeply loving relationship.

I can only hope that reading this play gives you as much pleasure as being part of the acclaimed London performance gave me.

Hayward Morse
London

PREFACE

Barry Morse: The Ultimate Shaw Specialist

Throughout the life and career of Barry Morse, his voice and presence as an actor, director and writer were ever-present somewhere around the world; and more often than not he was either telling those around him of Shaw, performing Shaw, or writing about Shaw. He was constantly building, encouraging, teaching, and carrying on the legacy of the great playwright. During the course of his career, whether on radio, television, or on-stage, Barry appeared in every play of George Bernard Shaw. He was, in many ways, the ultimate Shaw specialist.

As a student at the Royal Academy of Dramatic Art, Barry had the opportunity to meet and interact personally with Bernard Shaw on a number of occasions. One such encounter occurred during the production of Androcles and the Lion when Shaw came to an early student rehearsal of the play. Barry was cast in the pivotal role of the Lion and Shaw, dressed impeccably in his tailored tweed suit, lay down on the grubby rehearsal hall floor while waving his arms and legs in the air—to show Barry exactly how the Lion should react when, as Shaw told him, "he wants his tummy tickled."

After graduation, Barry performed in Shaw's Arms and the Man and Candida in repertory; followed by A Village Wooing in London's West End; which he thought was "wonderfully witty." After Barry and his family relocated to Canada in the early 1950s, Barry immediately found acting work there—his earliest performances included roles in The Philanderer and You Never Can Tell.

In 1959, Barry directed and starred in Shaw's Man and Superman in Boston with Rosemary Harris, just one of three productions of that play he headlined Massachusetts. Later, Barry served as Artistic Director of the famed Shaw Festival of Canada, where he spearheaded the expansion of the Festival to nine weeks and three full length plays— Man and Superman, Misalliance and The Apple Cart. On television, he continued to promote Shaw to wider audiences. Barry debuted Jerome Kilty's Dear Liar, with actress Zoe Caldwell (based on the letters of Shaw and the actress Mrs. Patrick Campbell); performed the voice of Shaw for a biographical film called George Bernard Shaw: Who The Devil Was He?; and traveled France where he appeared in the film The Wit and World of G. B. Shaw.

Barry was also cast in the world premiere of the complete Shaw play The Philanderer in London. The play was performed in 1992 for the first time with the fourth act intact, which, as Barry noted, "makes the play infinitely more satisfying." He debuted several new plays based on the life of Shaw, including Mollykins (based on the letters of the young would-be actress Molly Tompkins and Shaw); and Shavian Sextet, a piece about Shaw's works and his philosophies. Barry premiered my play Bernard and Bosie: A Most Unlikely Friendship (about the quite improbable relationship between George Bernard Shaw and Lord Alfred "Bosie" Douglas, the intimate friend of Oscar Wilde) in London, then then took it to Florida with his son, Hayward Morse.

One of his favorite latter-day roles was playing Bernard Shaw in the debut of The Private Life of George Bernard Shaw, by Elizabeth Sharland, the text of which is reproduced here for the first time. Barry was proud of his involvement with this ground-breaking play and performed it in both Toronto, Ontario, Canada and again in London, England at The Theatre Museum in Covent Garden. He enjoyed how the play examined Shaw's relationships with many of the women in his life, and the role itself required Barry to play Bernard Shaw at a number of different ages, from 29 to 94—while the women in Shaw's life were played by eight different actresses.

As co-author of his theatrical memoir Remember with Advantages, I feel I can speak confidently on Barry's behalf when I say he would be quite pleased to see the legacy of George Bernard Shaw continued through the availability of Elizabeth's play The Private Life of George Bernard Shaw in this book. Read and enjoy!

Anthony Wynn
May 5th 2011
New York City

Shaw in Love

The Private Life
of George Bernard Shaw

Elizabeth Sharland

CAST

George Bernard Shaw (GBS)
His mother
His sister (Lucy)
Alice Lockett
Jenny Patterson
Florence Farr
Janet Achurch
Ellen Terry
Mrs. Patrick Campbell
Beatrice Webb
Charlotte Payne Townsend

The stage is divided into four parts by the use of lighting. One section contains a desk and lamp, the second a table and chairs, the third a waiting room, and the fourth the lobby corner of the British Museum.

ACT ONE

GBS is seen standing centre stage. The stage is in darkness except for a spotlight above Shaw. He speaks to the audience.

GBS

To one biographer, I am a saint and an idealist; to another, a Don Juan with a woman in every theatre. My life has been hell, but because I kept the lid on, nobody has looked into it.

Women have been a ghastly nuisance in my life. My only real interests were writing and trying to make this world a better place to live in. Some biographers say I had twelve women, twelve relationships; however, most of the women I met did not measure up to my expectations, except two of them. I'll leave you to see for yourselves.

Lights fade

Area lit with table and chairs. Girl's voice is heard singing Gilbert and Sullivan's "A Wandering Minstrel I" with piano offstage.

GBS enters. He is carrying four books under one arm and a satchel in the other. His clothes are shabby and worn. He puts the books down on the table, takes off his coat, pours a glass of water from the decanter, opens satchel, takes out paper and begins to write. The music stops and voices are heard.

Enter GBS's mother and Alice Lockett talking together.

MA

Your work is progressing. Four lessons and you have improved enormously. Next week we will start on your lower register.

ALICE

I can't thank you enough, Mrs. Shaw. Your method really helps. Where did you find it?

MA

I learnt it in Dublin. That's one good thing to come out of that place. Hello, Sonny. You're home early. Alice, this is my son George.

GBS rises

GBS

How do you do.

ALICE

How do you do.

MA

This is Alice Lockett, a new pupil.

GBS

I was listening to you sing. You have a lovely voice.

ALICE

Thank you. I love singing Gilbert and Sullivan.

MA

You have a long journey home, Alice. Would you like a cup of tea before you go?

ALICE

Well, yes, yes, thank. I would like one very much.

MA

I'll get it then. George?

GBS

Yes please.

Ma goes out. There is a slight pause. During this conversation, both of them are shy and slightly embarrassed.

GBS

Please sit down.

ALICE

Do you like music - er - may I call you "George"?

GBS

Please do. Yes, mother taught me to sing and play the piano; however, I seldom do these days.

ALICE

Why not?

GBS

Too busy with other things.

ALICE

All those books. Are you a writer?

GBS

I'm working on it.

ALICE

What do you write?

GBS

Newspaper articles mainly.

ALICE

About what?

GBS

I review concerts, that kind of thing. I write music notices.

ALICE

A critic?

GBS

Sometimes.

ALICE

How interesting. You must attend many concerts.

GBS

I enjoy it and it is nice to be able to have free seats to most of them. What do you do?

ALICE

Nothing very exciting. I'm a nurse. I've just started at St Mary's Hospital in Paddington. Before that I was in training and trying to decide if I wanted to live in London. Oh yes. I teach Sunday School as well, on Sundays.

GBS

Of course, it would be Sunday, wouldn't it?

Both laugh.

ALICE

I love coming here to take lessons from your mother. She has a wonderful new method of teaching.

GBS

Do you want to become a professional singer then?

ALICE

No. I'm not good enough - it's just a hobby but it gives me something to do besides nursing. Would I have ready any of your reviews?

GBS

I doubt it. I write for small magazines and under an assumed name.

ALICE

Why?

GBS

It's easier. When I have one of my novels published I'll use my own name.

ALICE

How fortunate you are to have the time to write. I never seem to have the time to do anything but my job, except to practice my singing.

GBS

You don't go to any concerts?

ALICE

I can't AFFORD to. By the time I travel to London and pay my fares, there is nothing left

GBS

Do you like Handel's music?

ALICE

Yes, indeed. I have most of his music. My mother has a great library of musical scores. We used to go to concerts occasionally.

GBS

Perhaps you would like to come and hear some Handel next week. There is a concert at the Wigmore Hall next Thursday. I'll write and let you know if I will be reviewing it.

ALICE

How kind of you. Id love to go.

Blackout

Handel's piano music is heard as lights change to Shaw in spotlight again.

GBS

Alice, Alice, Alice, Alice. After that we used to meet at Liverpool Street Station. I waited for her in the waiting room. Each week we would meet in that frigid little room. I wrote to her, she wrote to me, every day. All I wanted to do was sit with her and watch those beautiful eyes at the end of a hard day of writing. Most young men throw themselves into the struggle for life. I threw my mother into it.

Blackout

Lights up on ma cleaning off the table and wiping it. She is humming Gilbert and

Sullivan. Enter GBS.

MA

You are late again. How many times have I told you to be home by six o'clock?

GBS

I was working and forgot the time.

MA

It is just not good enough. Your sister and I seem to do all the work here. You do nothing. You go out all day, and do precisely what you want. You have had three months holiday It is enough. You must settle down. You have to go out and find a job. You must work like everyone else.

GBS

But I am working.

MA

Working! You call mooning about sitting in the library at the British Museum working! We need money. You can't make any money sitting in the library every day. You must get a job.

GBS

I have an income from the reviews.

MA

It is not enough. Your work is not published. You write novels and nothing is accepted.

GBS

I need time.

MA

You've had enough time. I'm tired of supporting you. Look at you. You are 29 years old and you haven't a penny to bless yourself with. You should be thinking of settling down. I was married at your age with children. What girl is going to look at you if you can't support her?

GBS

It's only a matter of time.

MA

A matter of time. Well, perhaps you'd better go back to Dublin and live with your father, while you are waiting.

GBS

I'll never go back to Ireland.

MA

You may have to, if the money runs out in London.

GBS

Did Alice come today?

MA

No, she's ill. There is a letter there for you. Don't encourage her, Sonny, if you cannot be serious with her.

GBS

I'll read it in my room.

He exits ... enter Lucy Shaw, his sister... they cross on threshold.

MA

Oh dear, your brother will be the death of me!

LUCY

Well, you said you always wanted a boy. Sonny is a boy, or at least I think he is.

MA

He is a boy and always will be a boy. I don't think he will ever grow up. Look at him. He's nearly 30 and he has no job and no prospects. Writing novels ... nine years of it! And nothing.

LUCY

I think he's fond of Alice Lockett, don't you?

MA

Who knows?

LUCY

It would do him good to have a steady attachment. He would probably dress better and stop mooning about the British Museum. He is probably still innocent, don't you think?

MA

Lucy! Don't talk like that. You should know better.

LUCY

Well, what do you think, Ma? He is shy and he doesn't know what to say to girls. Perhaps it is all in his head.

MA

He is backward because his father is. That's why I left him.

LUCY

You left father because of his drinking.

MA

That's what I mean. He's backward. Always has been.

LUCY

Is he still sending us the money?

MA

Money! One pound a week, that's money? It's one pound less he can spend on drink.

LUCY

I miss him.

MA

You don't. You know you don't. You just imagine it.

LUCY

I wish Sonny was more like him. Father was always so cheerful and funny.

MA

Oh, I meant to tell you. He doesn't want to be called Sonny anymore. Especially in company. It is now "George". No pet names please.

LUCY

He is weird! Now he won't eat meat and now he won't touch alcohol. He is quite determined to forego the roast lamb for vegetables. He will become a head full of brains and underneath all woolly underwear and vegetables. Do you think he likes Alice?

MA

Enough of this. Off you go, you are wasting time.

Blackout

GBS in

Lights up on waiting room, Liverpool Street Station, sound of trains, train whistles, etc., voice announcements. GBS and Alice are seated on benches.

Voice over (GBS): "Time! Time! If I only I had more time!"

GBS

Alice, last night you were so intent to catch your train, you would not stay to hear my verse.

ALICE

I apologize. But George, you must stop writing these letters to me. My mother is objecting. It is too disturbing. You constantly flatter me! I am not so beautiful. I am not your dearest dear. I am not "your" Alice. I have never read such romantic fantasy as yours. You seem to imagine me as two women.

GBS

You are. Yes, Miss Lockett, all prim and conventional, formal and false; and then there is my dear Alice, my child, my lover, sympathetic and unspoiled.

ALICE

I'm not your lover. Don't say such things.

GBS

You could be. I wish you could be with me. We spend all our time meeting in railway stations or the British Museum.

ALICE

Well, we can't be alone at your mother's house.

GBS

We must value the time we have together, no matter where it is. Stay with me, don't catch your train. My days are full of work and I can't wait to be here to meet you. If I had your heart, of course, I know I should break it and yet I wish I had it. I don't like myself sometimes and sometimes I do not like you but there are moments when our two unfortunate souls seem to cling to the same star in a gleam of sunshine. Alice, Alice, Alice.

ALICE

Here's my train. I must go.

She kisses him on the cheek.

GBS

It was the same two nights ago Alice, how could you?

ALICE

Last night I understood we were to meet at 8.30 and I waited until 8.32 then distrust came into my heart and acting on nature I went straight home.

GBS

Well, I sat here, read a little, moped a little, hung about, watched the 9.30 train depart, went back to the waiting room, woke for the 10.10 train, and finally gave up. You were quite right to go by the 8.32. Had you waited I would have despised you for I respect people who always act sensibly and are devoid of the weaknesses known as "feelings". You behaved like a prudent woman, like a lady, and like a flint hearted wretch.

ALICE

How can you be so unkind? You insult me by telling me that I have nothing to do with the serious part of your life. You are in love with love, not with me. How many weeks have we been meeting like this? What for? So we can write love letters to each other? I believe you prefer writing and the act of composing love letters, rather than doing something about it. I will keep taking lessons from your mother, but we must end this flirtation. I have decided to become engaged to a doctor at the hospital who is far more realistic than you are. He is not a poet or a writer but he can take care of me and has a more mature love than yours. I plan to many him this spring. Goodbye, George. I shall miss my train.

She exits.

GBS recites poem "Alice"?

Blackout

Music: Gilbert and Sullivan. GBS in spotlight again.

GBS

My father died last week in Dublin. Now we have a letter from his lawyer enclosing eleven pounds for me. I decided I would spend the money on some new clothes. I went to Jaegers and bought a good wool suit. Wool is the healthiest material to wear next to the skin. Then some new boots and a cloak. From then on, women seemed to fall in love with me. Or maybe it was my new clothes! I no longer had to chase pretty women; they began to chase me. A short time later I first met Jenny Patterson. I met her in the same fashion as Alice. She is a widow and her husband seems to have disappeared from her memory completely. She has a worldly air about her and she started inviting me to her home in Brompton Square, which was certainly more comfortable than the railway station.

We played the piano together. Ah, the danger of a woman when she leans over the keyboard to turn the page. One night when I was playing some Handel variations, she leant over too far and I was completely captured. It was deliberate on her part I know! She seduced me on my 29th birthday. After that, I used to go to see her at least twice a week.

Lights up on both of them.

GBS

Be faithful to me.

JENNY

And you to me.

GBS

Do you want to hear my speech for Sunday's meeting?

JENNY

Have you finished it already?

GBS

Yes, and I am very nervous about the crowd.

JENNY

But surely most of your friends will be there to support you?

GBS

It is always a risk. I hope you will be there.

JENNY

Darling George, of course I will.

GBS

Last week I gave a speech at the Speakers Comer at Marble Arch in the pouring rain. No one came except six policemen who came to stop any rioting. They stood in their oilskins and listened to me for an hour. I can still see the light on their capes shining at me. I preached to them and they listened!

JENNY

You never talk to me about your friends. Do you have any?

GBS

You know about most of them.

JENNY

Who is Sydney Webb?

GBS

Sydney? Well, he is a plain, poor, earnest clerk from the Colonial Office. A bulky head set on a dumpy body. He looks like something between a London tradesman and a German professor. He knows everything I don't know - and I know everything he doesn't know. He is a political genius. He has the same idols as I have.

JENNY

And who are they?

GBS

Karl Marx and John Ruskin. Ruskin is a great artist, a philosopher - and yet he began as a painter. A lover of music, a poet, an economist and a socialist. Sydney Webb puts all their ideas down on paper and I shall be their spokesman.

JENNY

So Webb is the partner in all your new socialism?

GBS

Yes. The WEBB-SHAW machine could replace Marx as the most powerful force in British socialism. Webb really is the inventor of Fabian Socialism.

JENNY

And who is Sydney Olivier?

GBS

He is another genius.

JENNY

What does he do?

GBS

He works as a clerk in the Colonial office too. He and Webb and I will be speaking on Sunday.

JENNY

The three of you! Imagine trying to change the world. The Fabians!

GBS

We can do it

JENNY

The Three Musketeers"! The three Fabian musketeers!

GBS

I must go and finish the speech.

JENNY

But if Webb is writing it...

GBS

And I must rally up more friends.

JENNY

Who is Annie Besant?

GBS (*looks shocked*)

Annie Besant?

JENNY

She is in the Fabian Society, is she not?

GBS

Yes she is. But I've not met her. She is a disciple of Ibsen. You know, she was trying to write a sequel to "A Doll's House."

JENNY

Gossip has it that she has left her husband. A clergyman. Not only that, but she walked out of their home and the church. She refused to believe in Christianity and refused to take the sacrament. There was an article in the paper this morning about her. All her beliefs were reported and they condemned her.

GBS

She is a "new" woman. She is one of the group who are going to get the vote for women. She will change so much for women.

JENNY

Ha. Does she support herself? How does she live? What is so wonderful about these "new" women? They will push hard enough to get the vote, then what? They will want to start wearing the trousers of you men. She probably left her husband for another man.

GBS

Jenny! Don't talk of something you know nothing about.

JENNY

Well, if you would spend half the time writing your own work, your novels and your plays, instead of writing all this political stuff, you might get something published.

How are you ever going to get one of your plays produced in London, if you go on about your political beliefs? Darling George. How long have we known each other? Two years? And you must believe me, you are too serious, you work too hard. Come and eat and make love. Make love to me.

They embrace. Lights fade. Shaw in spotlight, giving speech.

GBS

Capitalism breeds slavery! Your slaves are beyond caring, they breed like rabbits and their poverty breeds filth, ugliness, dishonesty, disease, obscenity, drunkenness and murder. In the midst of the riches which they labor piles up for you, their misery rises up too and stifles you. You withdraw in disgust to the other end of the town from them. You appoint special seats in your churches and theatres for them. You set your life apart from theirs by every class barrier you can devise, and yet they swarm about you still. Under cover of protecting my person and property you forcibly take my money to support an army of soldiers and policemen for the execution of barbarous and detestable laws.

Noise of audience. Cheers and boos. Applause. A woman runs up to Shaw.

It is Annie Besant.

ANNIE

Here! Here! Bravo. My name is Annie Besant. You must come and march to Trafalgar Square. We are all going next Sunday. We must march. You must be there!

Here we are next Sunday in Trafalgar Square. Noise of riots. Police sirens. Shouts, banners and flag is marched across the stage. Loud cries and screams. Annie runs on after Shaw enters. His face is bloody.

ANNIE

Why did you run away? We had reached Trafalgar Square.

GBS

It's no use. We can't fight against policemen armed with truncheons and coshes, it's madness. Look, I was hit in the face. Police are everywhere. Webb has been arrested. I do not want to be killed, or even put in prison.

ANNIE

If I can do it, so can you! *(She pulls him)*.

GBS

Annie, go home. You must not try to march again.

ANNIE

George Bernard Shaw, you are a coward!

GBS

I'm just being sensible. Look at your arm! *(Blood)*.

ANNIE

Come to the meeting tomorrow night. I will bring more supporters. We must follow through. Next Sunday we march again ...

GBS

It is utter folly. Expecting an unarmed, undisciplined multitude to prevail against trained, disciplined soldiers and policemen!

ANNIE

We must do what has to be done!

GBS

Annie, I love you. I love your ideals but we must be careful. Come, let me take you home.

Blackout.

Music, Handel

Lights up on Annie now writing at her desk. She reads what she has written.

ANNIE

Darling George. You call me sexless! Sexless! Ha! This is not true. Don't bait me. The only relationship I want with you must be a legitimate one. Even though the Trafalgar Square march was only three months ago, you know how I feel about your philandering. If you want me, and me alone, then we will have to be married. Oh, not in the Christian sense, because I am still a married woman. I have at last, after many sleepless nights, reached a conclusion. If we still want to continue to be with each other, we must obey society's wishes. Last week you agreed that I should compose a marriage contract between us, and this is what I have done. I am enclosing a copy of the draft which contains all the conditions of our marriage contract. Naturally, there will be no marriage ceremony in any religious place of worship or in any registry office as I am still married. Here is the draft We can marry ourselves.

Fade out. Lights up on Shaw.

GBS

Good God! This is worse than all the vows exacted by all the churches on earth! You cannot expect my signature. I'd rather be legally married to you ten times over. Love! Romance! That way madness lies.

And now another problem Jenny comes to our house for mother's lessons, and if mother is late ... Jenny has access to my room and she goes there, and reads my letters Jenny!

JENNY

(VERY ANGRY) You are a black villain! Annie Besant indeed! No matter that one act of unfaithfulness is as bad as a hundred. How could you? After such lips and kisses as mine! Anyway, if you are unfaithful to me, let it be with someone nice, not that horrid looking woman. Do you know how I feel? After ten months of intimacy? Have pity on me. I have some right to ask it from you. Do not abandon me. I can't help wanting to see you.

GBS

Jenny, please give me back the letters.

JENNY

Why should I? They belong to me just as much as you. You are my lover, not hers. If you cheat me, then you cheat yourself. How could you write such letters to someone else?

GBS

Your vanity is hurt.

JENNY

Vanity! I think my vanity suffers very little. I regret your indifference because you have not only been a lover but a friend. *(Softly)* I can't help wanting to see you. You are so much to me. I am so happy when I am with you. You are the one man in all the world to me. *(Changes to rage)*. Annie Besant. How could you?

GBS

She believes in the same justice as I do.

JENNY

Don't talk about justice to me. The same causes, perhaps. But that's no reason to go to bed with her. She is a mad woman. Unbalanced. She has no personal loyalty at all. She would probably drop you as she did her husband and family.

GBS

I forbid you to speak of her like this.

JENNY

Forbid! She is a horrid creature. She causes riots in the streets. Bloodshed! You could have been killed by one blow from that policeman. I will never forget the trouble she caused that Sunday in Trafalgar Square. Bloody Sunday they call it. For what? For Fabianism! Is it worth your life? Now she is saying that you ran away.

GBS

Enough. Enough. Please leave me. I have work to do. Give me the letters. *(He goes to her.)*

JENNY

Promise you won't see her again!

GBS

I can't promise that. We WORK together.

JENNY

Ha! Work together. That is what you call it. I will not tolerate your unfaithfulness, it is either her or me. You know she is using you. She doesn't love you, she loves herself, and her ideals. She will drop you and your friends if you don't follow her. Come to your senses for God's sake. Here! Take her letters. *(She throws them at him.)*

GBS

Please just leave me alone.

JENNY

(Sitting down) Leave you alone! After all I have done for you! The trouble is that you have forgotten who you are and where you came from. Your father was a drunken peasant who couldn't support his family. Just because your mother is a music teacher of great talent, you think you

can aspire to the artistic and cultural life in London. Now that you have met Annie Besant, who is a celebrity in your eyes, you will use her! I can see right through you. I am no longer any use to you. You have used me in every sense of the word and when you meet the next useful woman Annie Besant will be dropped as well.

GBS

Have you finished?

JENNY

I have seen what you do. You deceived me too. What a seducer you are!

GBS

Madam, I must correct you. I recall it was the other way round.

JENNY

Go to hell You USE women for material. You used me for your writing. Used my emotion. My love for you. You will use all my emotion for your plays!

GBS

Why not? I'll use it if you will give it to me.

JENNY

Not bloody likely! (She exits).

Spotlight on Shaw

GBS

I go about in search of love. When I try to ask for it, this horrible shyness strangles me, and I stand dumb, or worse than dumb, saying meaningless things, foolish lies. I am longing for affection. I give it to cats and dogs and pet birds because they come and ask for it. It must be asked for. It is like a ghost. It would speak, but it dare not, because it is shy, shy, shy! That is the world's tragedy. Quite by accident I met the most charming woman last night. Florence Farr. "Florence!" The very name conjures up beauty. She had read my play.

We spoke about the theatre and after several minutes I knew she was an actress.

FLORENCE

I must tell you how much I enjoyed reading your play, "Widower's Houses" Mr Shaw.

GBS

It certainly seems to be fate that we should meet I wanted to write to you and congratulate you on your. "Rosmersholm" Ibsen is obviously the best playwright to be introduced in London this year.

FLORENCE

I am not sure. I like your plays just as well.

GBS

Thank you for the compliment.

FLORENCE

I know that you are a busy man so I will be brief. I have a mentor who is a friend of the family. However, she doesn't wish to be named because of possible disapproval from her family, but she has recently given an amount of money to enable me to rent a theatre in London and present a season of new plays. The plays must be by new playwrights.

GBS

May I ask who has been so generous?

FLORENCE

She has sworn me to secrecy. Her family do not approve of the theatre, and her gift must be kept secret. As I said, I like your play and I would hope you would allow me to play the lead in it.

GBS

If that is what you wish.

FLORENCE

Good! Then it is settled. We will produce the play next month and start rehearsals next week. Do you want to direct it?

GBS

Of course, if that is agreeable.

FLORENCE

I am honored to be the first person to introduce your plays in London. My father, William Farr, admires your reviews and your work in the political world tremendously. He always wanted me to be a teacher, but he now realizes I have always wanted to be in the theatre. Last year we both met Yeats, your fellow countryman, but he writes completely differently. You two are completely different.

GBS

We are!

FLORENCE

Shaw, the socialist, and Yeats, the mystic. Shaw the anti-romantic, and Yeats the true romantic.

GBS

And what about you? Where is your husband? In Ireland?

FLORENCE

No, he was not Irish.

GBS

Is he dead then?

FLORENCE

No, he is in America.

GBS

America!

FLORENCE

He is dead as far as I'm concerned. I married an actor and when he couldn't find work here, he left me and went to America where I hear he has been very successful. After living at home for so long I relish my freedom. I want to present and act in new plays, plays with contemporary issues and political ideals.

GBS

I am working on another such a play. It's called "ARMS AND THE MAN".

FLORENCE

Well, quickly finish it, and we will present it immediately. Yeats has a new play, but it's a short one, so we could do that as a curtain raiser for yours.

GBS

I would like to direct all the plays myself.

FLORENCE

Then you shall, Mr. Shaw, you shall.

GBS (*moves to centre*)

Sometime later I met another actress, Janet Achurch. It was at a party. And in the matter of partying Janet was prone to party, not wisely, but too well.

They are at a party, standing up, eating with forks off plates. Voices, chatter, music in background.

JANET *(slightly intoxicated)*

Good evening, you are Mr. Shaw, are you not?

GBS

Correct, and you?

JANET

My name is Janet, Janet Achurch ... I'm an actress in Herbert Tree's company at the Haymarket.

GBS

Ah, yes, of course. You are Nora in "A DOLL'S HOUSE".

JANET

You've seen it?

GBS

Of course. You were marvelous.

JANET

Thank you. Coming from you that is a real compliment.

GBS

The role might have been written for you. You were brilliant.

JANET

It is a wonderful play.

GBS

With a wonderful actress.

GBS

Where are you from?

JANET

Manchester. My grandparents were once the managers of the Theatre Royal, so I was brought up by them in the theatre. Mr. Shaw, I do hope I can work for you. I have read everything you have written.

GBS

Have you my dear. Well, I believe you could play anything.

JANET

Try me!

GBS

I'm coming to see the play again tomorrow night. Perhaps we can have dinner afterwards.

JANET

Dinner, breakfast, whatever! Why don't we run away together?

GBS

Why not indeed!

JANET

You could write marvelous plays for me.

GBS

Indeed.

JANET

You would be sick of me in a week.

GBS

That implies you could entertain me for a week. Good heavens, with what?

JANET

What indeed!

GBS

Art, politics, philosophy? I've written more about them for a living than you ever thought about them.

JANET

Maybe I have knowledge of a different kind.

GBS

Some day, when you have two hours to spare, you must let me read you my new play, "CANDIDA". I must always read it, you see, then you can hear the audience sobbing at least three streets off.

JANET

We are taking "A DOLL'S HOUSE" to Australia next week. It was part of our contract.

GBS

Ah. Then all is lost.

JANET

Would I could stay here and fall in love with you.

GBS

Ha! Ha! What a fine idea.

JANET

I think I already am.

GBS

So soon?

JANET

So soon. I look forward to tomorrow night.

Fade to Shaw

GBS

Kindly consider that for years past every Sunday evening of mine has been spent on some more or less squalid platform, lecturing, lecturing, lecturing. But just imagine the effect of being suddenly magnetized, irradiated, transported, fired, rejuvenated, bewitched, by a wild and glorious woman. That night I stayed up till 2 am writing to her.

"Dear Janet, The world has vanished, the gardens of heaven surround me. I thought I was old, that youth was gone, that I should never be in love again in the starry way of the days before the great disillusion. And lo! It is all back again, with the added wisdom to know my own happiness. I desire nothing, I hope for nothing, I covet nothing. I possess, enjoy, exult. Away with you to Australia - forever, if you will. See whether that prospect will dash me one job! Change, fade, become a mere actress, or simply amuse yourself by ruthless and careless manslaughter."

JANET

Was ever woman in such fashion wooed? - by a vegetarian who dined, ever on the run, on apples, nuts, macaroni, brown bread, and cocoa; who penned articles in suburban train carriages while travelling to and from Socialist lecture engagements or theatrical performances (occasionally losing his manuscripts under the wheels as he emerged at his station), or who scribbled plays in shorthand in pocket notebooks at odd moments, leaning against the Embankment, standing beneath a fog-shrouded gas lamp at a street corner at midnight, sprawled beside his bicycle in a country meadow surrounded by cud-chewing bovines, or seated nonchalantly on a park bench under an umbrella in pouring rain.

Back and forth he darted each afternoon and evening, from the Fabian office in the Strand to the British Museum reading room, pouring over government "blue books" and researching on local drainage or on public lavatories in his capacity as a newly elected Vestryman of the Parish of St Pancras. Then off again to the theatre or a meeting, returning finally, after a brisk night walk, to his study in Fitzroy Square. There he worked until the small hours of the morning under the flickering light of a reading lamp, while his eyes smarted and teared, until the pain drove him to resort to an eyeshade or sunglasses, and to the use of green-tinted, non-glare paper for his manuscripts and correspondence. And when he had difficulty walking in the morning (even the alarm couldn't rouse him), he impatiently accused himself of laziness! But then, I hardly ever saw him because he was deep in rehearsals with Florence Farr.

(In rehearsal)**FARR**:I would marry the man I loved which no other Queen in Europe has the courage to do.

GBS

No! No! No! No! Not like that. I can't hear you! You must project! Your voice is terrible. Leave everyone, go home. I will talk to Miss Farr alone. Go on, leave.

FLORENCE

I can't believe you could be so cruel.

GBS

Don't be stupid. I'm not cruel. I just want to be able to hear you.

FLORENCE

Then TEACH ME! I have never been so humiliated. Nobody ever shouts at me. Teach me, if you know how.

GBS

You must go to a voice coach. Go to Herbert Tree. Tree is the best coach in London. He will teach you phonetically.

FLORENCE

Phonetically?

GBS

He has a new method. What's the use of acting if people can't hear you?

FLORENCE

Maybe it's you. Maybe you are deaf. Yeats doesn't have any trouble hearing me.

GBS

Well, you go to Herbert Tree and I will be contented. What's the use of my writing plays if they cannot be heard?

FLORENCE

Don't be angry with me, please. I am trying. You must not bully me. Please.

GBS

You call me a bully? There is nothing that drives me to such utter despair as when I make some blundering and unsuccessful attempt to make you see some theatrical point that my mother can teach to any idiot in a few lessons. You do not know the importance of some of these tricks as regards health, economy of physical force, self-contentedness, and the like. All mat it is necessary for you to do is to say my lines so clearly that the audience can understand every word.

FLORENCE

What about my acting?

GBS

As long as they can hear my lines, you can act or not, as you please.

FLORENCE *(tearfully)*

Please. Please. Look, I will become you student. Rehearse me. Teach me. I will do want you want. But this season must be successful. (She goes to him). I admire you tremendously and I think I am in love with you.

GBS

You are a sweet girl who romanticizes too much. I'm sorry if I upset you.

FLORENCE

Come, kiss me. Let's get it over with. I always hate the shyness of a first kiss. . (She pulls him into an embrace. They kiss). There now. It's over. You know, whenever I want to make love I feel as if I am in a role. I'm on stage! I become an actress, acting out a part. Have you ever had an affair with an actress?

GBS

I do not have "affairs". Women are too dangerous.

FLORENCE

Then who is Jenny Patterson?

GBS *(Surprised)*

Why do you ask about her?

FLORENCE

Because she came to the theatre yesterday after you had gone and demanded to see you.

GBS

Well, she's not an actress. The woman is a hysteric. She feels I owe her something.

FLORENCE

Do you?

GBS

Not at all. She just wants all the letters she wrote me. We were friends some time ago.

FLORENCE

I don't really want to see her again, if that's possible. Could you tell her not to come to the theatre again please.

GBS

I will. But it won't do any good.

FLORENCE

So many women seem to admire you and yet I've never heard you say a good word about any of them. Is there any woman you admire besides Annie Besant?

GBS

There are many.

FLORENCE

Name one.

GBS

Queen Victoria!

FLORENCE

Queen Victoria!

GBS

Queen Victoria! For example, we all know that she has been of all the wives the best, of all mothers the fondest, of all widows the most faithful. We have often seen her, despite her lofty station, moved by famines, colliery explosions, shipwrecks, and railway accidents, thereby teaching us that a heart beats in her Royal breast as in the humblest of her subjects.

FLORENCE

Are you going to see Jenny Patterson and stop her coming to the theatre?

GBS

Yes. It is done. Jenny Patterson is merely infatuated with me. Anyone who becomes the object of infatuation shrinks from it instinctively. Love loses its charm when it is not free. Like the caresses of a maniac. The successful wooer, in both sexes alike, is the one who can stand out for honorable conditions and, failing them, go without. I shall become your tutor. You must work. Bunch up your body and stiffen your neck. We must work as we cross the Himalayas to make you a leading lady!

Blackout

Mrs. Shaw is seen mixing flour in a mixing bowl. Flour on her hands.

MA

You only come home when you need clean clothes. WE never see you. Lucy has been ill for a week and you didn't even know. Where are you going this weekend?

GBS

Down to Gloucestershire.

MA

Again?

GBS

It is good to get out of London.

MA

That's all right for you. Why don't you think about us for a while.

GBS

I do. I do. But rehearsals have been going on day and night. How can I help you when I am exhausted.

MA

And now the gossip! People are talking about you and May Morris. She is a married woman, Sonny. You can't keep going down to the country and staying with a married couple. It isn't correct.

GBS

(Sitting down) Her husband doesn't mind. He says he gets better meals when I'm there.

MA

She is still a married woman. Her husband must resent you.

GBS

Not at all. We all go for long walks, play the piano, talk, and I keep them both entertained. I need the break.

MA

Where are you going tonight?

During this scene Shaw removes his socks, takes a clean pair, uses them to demonstrate his speech, puts them on and slowly finishes his dressing.

GBS

To the opera at Covent Garden.

MA

You can't go to Covent Garden like that!

GBS

Why not? I went last week.

MA

And you were turned away you told me.

GBS

Well, I wrote to the manager to complain. He will have got my letter by now. I told him that next season I shall purchase a stall for the most important evening I can select. I shall dress in white flannels. I shall then hire for the evening the most repulsive waiter I can find in the lowest oyster shop in London. I shall rub him with bacon crackling, smooth his hair with fried sausages, shower stale gravy upon him, season him with Worcester Sauce, and give him just enough drink to make him assertive without making him actually drunk. With him I shall present myself at the stalls, explain that he is my brother and that we have arranged that I am to see the opera, unless evening dress is indispensable, in which case my brother, being in evening dress, must take my place.

MA

Honestly, George. How can you write such letters?

GBS

Oh, I have another one. ha! which is even better! Now here, where is it? Ah yes, here it is this is my review for THE STAR of a sermon preached by the bishop of Rochester. It's in the form of a letter from a Cockney case monger.

(Reads with an accent)

"Honored Sir and Editor, Having bin for the first time in my life to church for to hear the Bishop of Rochester preach I take the liberty of letting you know what passed, thinking that perhaps you never seen a Bishop and no more had I till this very evening. He sat to the left of the table that was railed in to put the money on (we all settin well outside with the singers all in white between us and it). The Bishop had a red. . . . . . and was as hard as nails and proper stiff, I can tell you. He saved himself up for the sermon, and the boys sung a sam like mad, cutting out the running for the organ, which done a good finish, the organ had windows, and the gentleman kept opening and shutting them so that sometimes you couldn't hear yourself and sometimes you couldn't hear him. The singing was the best of it to my taste, then the

Bishop he up a ladder and preached about socialism; but he warnt used to it, and when I sez "Here, here" to encourage him, he stops and sez: "This is a church" sez he, as if I didn't know, it was a treat to hear him giving everybody a what for all round. Then he give it to the police, and said Christ hadn't nothing to do with them, then he give it to the capitalists and said they must all be done away with. Then he give it to us for cheering him. Then he says: "Blessed are ye poor; for yours is the Kingdom of Heaven." then he says, quite genteel, as he hoped he worn't wearying us; but we was bashful to answer, afraid he'd give it to us again. Then he takes a snooze for about forty winks with his head in his hands; and we sings a hymn very quiet, so as not to wake him. Then he hears the money chinking, and comes down the ladder prompt to take it at the table. Then he blesses us as if the whole place belonged to him; and out we sneaks hot foot I must say I never see a man come up more to my notion of a Bishop as him. I wish I was one. I am, Sir, yours respectfully, Jem Nicholls,.

PS the church was the big un in the Waterloo Road, near the railway bridge.

I seem to have something of a facility for this cockney lingo perhaps I could do something more along those lines. Perhaps a story about a cockney flower give named Eliza Doolittle.

Music up. "My Fair Lady

Act Two

GBS

Women! All these women are going mad! Florence has joined the GOLDEN DAWN SOCIETY! A group that studies magic! To study and practice magic. GOLDEN DAWN. I ask you.

Annie Besant has become a theosophist!

My mother has taken to the ouija board. She wants messages from my dead relatives.

Janet has become an alcoholic and is taking morphia and now this latest actress Elizabeth Robins has threatened to shoot me! (Exit)

Knock on the door. Mrs. Shaw goes to door. Beatrice Webb enters.

BEATRICE

Good afternoon, Mrs. Shaw. I am Beatrice Webb. I am a friend of George's. I came to call on him. Is he home?

MA

No, I'm sorry, he is not here. Won't you come in anyway?

BEATRICE

Thank you. Do you know where he might be?

MA

Probably in the reading room at the British Museum. Would you like some tea?

BEATRICE

No thank you. You are very kind. I feel I'm intruding.

MA

Not at all. Please sit down. I've heard so much about you and your husband. It is very good of you to invite my son down at the weekends.

BEATRICE

My husband, Sydney, works with the Fabian Society as well. George has enabled us to expand and promote our society a great deal.

MA

He seems to have forgotten about his other work and goes on and on about his political views. I don't know what will become of him.

BEATRICE

We haven't heard from him for some time. Is he all right?

MA

He was away for a while and he has been ill. His foot became infected last wcck and it is not healing.

BEATRICE

His foot?

MA

Evidently, he had a large blister from wearing a new size boot and it became infected and now he can hardly walk.

Door slams offstage

Ah, that's him. I'll call him as he usually goes straight up to his room. I never see him. *(She calls out)* George, come in. You have a visitor.

GBS

enters. He is on crutches.

BEATRICE

George, how are you? We were wondering how you were.

GBS

Hello, Beatrice, it's good to see you.

BEATRICE

Goodness me! *(Sees crutches).* We had no idea you were in this state. What happened?

GBS

It's nothing really. My foot became infected last week and it hasn't got any better.

BEATRICE

Have you seen a doctor?

GBS

Briefly, yes.

MA

He told him to rest it. Yet he keeps walking around London in all that filth. What can one do?

GBS

Please don't fuss over me. It will heal eventually.

BEATRICE

Do you have a dressing on it?

GBS

Yes, and lots of ointment.

MA

Well, I'll leave the two of you to talk. I have things to do. It was a pleasure meeting you, Mrs. Webb. Please call again whenever you are in this area.

BEATRICE

Thank you. You are very kind.

Ma goes out.

GBS

All I need is a few days off my feet.

BEATRICE

Perhaps a wheelchair?

GBS

No, not that.

BEATRICE

Have you seen the papers?

GBS

What about?

BEATRICE

All the riots. It's Annie Besant again.

GBS

Yes, I told her I was not going to participate in any more marches. She will not stop, you know, till they put her in prison. I haven't got the time. I have too much work to do.

BEATRICE

By the way, I think I have found you a secretary. She's willing to do all your typing for you.

GBS

Who is she?

BEATRICE

Her name is Charlotte, Charlotte Payne Townsend. She's from Ireland. In fact, she is a very wealthy woman who is alone in London but needs something to do. I have invited her down for the weekend. If you can manage it, we will send a carriage for you.

GBS

What is she like?

BEATRICE

A charming woman. She has spent the last few months in Italy and has just taken a flat nearby in Adelphi Terrace.

GBS

Attractive?

BEATRICE

Well, you can see for yourself this weekend.

GBS

I can give her work immediately.

BEATRICE

Good, then that's one problem solved. Then there is another, far more serious.

GBS

What's that?

BEATRICE

Bertha Newcombe.

GBS

Bertha?

BEATRICE

She asked me to visit her yesterday.

GBS

I didn't even know you knew her.

BEATRICE

She wrote me a letter last week and begged me to go to her studio. Sydney and I knew you were involved with Jenny, Florence and Janet, but I didn't know about Bertha. She told me everything, it was a terrible time for her. She really loves you. I had no idea she was painting your portrait and that you had been there so constantly all these months. George, what are you going to do? Do you realize she expects you to marry her? What will you do? I saw the portrait. It is brilliant. She has captured you exactly.

GBS

I've already told her I can't marry her. I was going to tell you and Sydney about her.

BEATRICE

The poor woman is desperate. What can we do?

GBS

Nothing. I broke it off because she was expecting too much.

BEATRICE

She said you had been there every day-for weeks.

GBS

It's over. I can't do anything more for her. Besides, she knew I would never marry her.

BEATRICE

I promised her I'd talk to you about it.

GBS

I'll write to her again and explain.

BEATRICE

Please do, or go and see her. Why won't you marry her?

GBS

First of all because I don't love her and, secondly, you know my views on marriage.

BEATRICE

But that view is based on our discussion about marrying a wealthy woman. Bertha is not wealthy.

GBS

Exactly.

BEATRICE

You mean you would only marry a wealthy woman?

GBS

Don't be ridiculous. I would never submit myself. Marriage for property is prostitution and do you think I would sell myself? I would become the prostitute in a relationship. Do you think Bertha would care if I was wealthy or not...

BEATRICE

Go to her, at least talk to her.

GBS

I can't like this. Don't worry. I'll write to her. Last week I had a letter from Ellen Terry ...

BEATRICE

Ellen Terry? The actress?

GBS

Yes, to ask my opinion of her protégé, a young singer. I went to her concert but she had no talent, which I told Miss Terry in my letter. She replied to me today and I've written back to her.

BEATRICE

Perhaps you could send one of your plays to her.

GBS

In time, yes, in time.

BEATRICE

It is a good idea if she could act in one of your plays. Why don't you ask her if she will read one?

GBS

Let's wait and see if she replies to my letter.

BEATRICE

Well, I must go. Don't get up. I can let myself out. Let me know if you can come.

Fade out. Spotlight on Shaw

GBS

Dear Miss Terry,

Thank you for your kind letter. I am enclosing a copy of my play "MAN OF DESTINY" for your perusal. Of course, I would be prepared to offer it to Mr. Irving, provided you would be prepared to play in it. Please advise. Please do not even consider cutting the play. It is bad enough to do that to Shakespeare, but its sacrilege to cut Shaw.

ELLEN

I am exceedingly obliged to you for troubling yourself so much about my little friend. Your letter saddened me very much, for I do care for the girl, and long and long to help her. She's so alone, and so very, very little assertive. She HAS individuality; and I learn every day from her simplicity. But I see a peep hole in your words for Blessed Hope. I will work to get her a few lines on the stage for a few shillings a week and at least then she will know the great happiness of occupation. I didn't like you when you first wrote to me. I thought you unkind, and exceedingly stiff and prim. Now I beg your pardon most heartily. Although, of course, it matters no jot to you what I think, I must yet ask you to take my best bestest thanks for your long last splendid letter, and believe me most gratefully yours...Ellen

GBS

Dear Miss Terry, You signed yourself Ellen, so does this mean we are now firm friends? Thank you for your kind letter. Ellen Terry is the most beautiful name in the world. It rings like a chime through the last quarter century. It has a lovely rhythm in it. I am, and always have been, and ever shall be, by preeminent brevity and commonsense, simply, Shaw

ELLEN

Just read your play. Delicious! Irving loves it, and will do it finely.

GBS

Befriend me to the extent of letting me know seriously whether Irving wishes me to hold the play for him..

ELLEN

I wish you two were friends, that you knew each other. I don't want you to know me, for I'm such a fool you'd be sick of me in a week - and that would be hateful - but Henry is different. You'd love him. He can do everything except be fond of people, but that's his great misfortune.

GBS

What is this? He will not do my play until next December? Do you suppose I will let him treat me as he treats Shakespeare - play me centuries after I am dead? Is he blind, is he deaf... that he passes by the great chances of his life as if they were pieces of orange peel laid in his path expressly to capsize him? This week I will be forty! I expect an offer. You are only playing with me. I will go to that Beautiful Mrs. Patrick Campbell. SHE shall play the Strange Lady. Farewell, faithless Ellen.

ELLEN

You ARE in the blues! You are only a boy. Forty is NOTHING when it's Irish! Be strong. Don't waste your time on any woman. Shake the world, you stupid darling. Give up picture sitting, writing to elderly actresses (selfish beasts). Give up fooling. It's only because you are a boy, but it's not fair. It's horrid, and like a flirting girl who is more thoughtless, maybe, than wicked. But at forty you ought to have felt the ache of it. I guess you have given the ache to this poor lady, and you couldn't do that if you knew the pain. But, you're only a boy.

She exits.

GBS

I certainly did not give up writing to elderly actresses. But my dear, dear Ellen was no elderly actress then. However, nothing prevented us from writing to each other because I adored her.

Lights up on Lucy and GBS.

LUCY

I must ask you to move up to your room. Mother is expecting a new student and she will need this room. What did the doctor say?

48

GBS

He warned me that I may have to have my toe amputated. The infection is not healing.

LUCY

What a business. You can't go on like this; something has to be done. You must obey the doctor's orders. You have to eat some liver to improve your blood.

GBS

LIVER? So life is offered to me on condition of eating meat? Death is better than cannibalism. Do you know, Lucy, when I die my will contains directions for my funeral, which will be followed not by mourning coaches, but by herds of oxen, sheep, swine, flocks of poultry and a small travelling aquarium of live fish, all wearing white scarves in honor of the man who perished rather than eat his fellow creatures. It will be, with the exception of the procession into Noah's Ark, the most remarkable thing of the kind ever seen.

LUCY

Get away with you.

Doorbell rings. Charlotte Payne Townsend enters.

CHARLOTTE

Excuse me. I hope I'm not intruding. Hullo. I'm Charlotte Payne Townsend. You must be Lucy.

LUCY

Hullo. Yes, please come in. Are those more papers for George?

CHARLOTTE

Yes, I've finished them. Hullo, Mr. Shaw.

GBS

Hullo.

LUCY

Perhaps you could help him to his room. My mother has a student arriving shortly.

CHARLOTTE

Come on Mr. Shaw. Let me help you up the stairs.

Exit

CHARLOTTE

I was appalled. He worked in a very small room which was in a perpetual state of dirt and disorder. He kept the window wide open, day and night, winter and summer, and the dust and smuts that entered thereby settled on the books, furniture and papers, then being scattered over a wider area whenever attempts were made to remove them, the mass of matter on the table was chaotic! Heaps of letters, pages of manuscripts, books, envelopes, writing paper, pens ... butter, sugar, apples, knives, forks, spoons, sometimes a cup of cocoa or a half-finished plate of porridge, a saucepan, and a dozen other things, were mixed up indiscriminately and all undusted, as his papers must not be touched. The table, the typewriter and the wooded-railed chair in which he sat filled the room, forcing anyone who entered it to move sideways like a crab. As he read books while he was dressing and undressing and deposited them, open, on the table without bothering to shut them, there was a fair state of chaos. His mother never comes into the room, and they did not have their meals together. When his mother was in for a meal, the servant brought in a plateful of cooked eggs and put them down on the nearest pile of books and papers. I knew something had to be done! *(Exits)*.

GBS

It was planned I must go away to the country the moment I could be moved, and that somebody must seriously take in hand the job of looking after me. Charlotte was the inevitable and predestined agent appointed by destiny. She took a house for me to convalesce in and in order to save her reputation I sent her out for a marriage license and a ring. I was hardly in a physical condition to go out and get them myself. I found that my own objection to my marriage had ceased with my objection to my own death. So it was planned I must go to the country. One of the subjects we discussed was money. I was not making enough money to support Charlotte in the manner to which she was accustomed and if I left Fitzroy Square mother would not be able to manage on the fees she earned from teaching music. So Charlotte settled an annuity on my mother for life. When I went back to Fitzroy Square after our wedding and broke the news to my mother she made no comment beyond saying that it was 'not unexpected'. She supposed that she must call Miss Payne Townsend "Charlotte" now, though "Carlotta" was rather more descriptive. She looked a Carlotta. Mother had taken to Ouija boards and séances and had ideas on the unseen forces beyond the material world.

We were married on June 1st in a registry office in Covent Garden. It was pouring with rain. Of the two witnesses we had, Sydney Olivier, who was much better dressed man I, was mistaken for the groom and because of my rather shabby attire, I was thought of as someone off the street who'd been called in as a witness. This prompted Charlotte to start buying me new clothes. I was a married man at last

After much searching, we secured this house. I came down on crutches. The air was so fine that our troubles seemed over: but they had only just begun. The moment I began to get strong I recklessly began to work on a book about Wagner. After dictating Wagner criticism for half an hour I called a halt and went up to get something from my bedroom. Coming down, the crutches shot me into the air. I snatched the banister on the landing above and caught it in my right hand but it snapped and I fell 50 fathoms to the floor with my left arm underneath me. Charlotte made me a splint and I lay there till the doctor came. Then, last night, a cat, shut up accidentally in the pantry, simulated a burglar so successfully that I sallied out, walking recklessly, at 3 in the morning and fell again. I now have a wheelchair, as you see.

CHARLOTTE

Who are you writing to? Ha, need I ask?

GBS

Dear Charlotte, You know I have never met her.

CHARLOTTE

I know, but George, we must have no secrets from each other. Now we have discussed all our previous past lives. What do I have to know about all these actresses, most of all Ellen?

GBS

She is an angel, but you must believe, our correspondence means more to me, and to her, than if we were to meet.

CHARLOTTE

She must help you with your plays.

GBS

I am to see Irving this week and discuss the production.

CHARLOTTE

After that, can we go abroad?

GBS

I hate to travel. If we must go, please wait till my play has opened.

CHARLOTTE

Your mother wants to come for the weekend.

GBS

Why don't you go away with her-

CHARLOTTE

No. She doesn't really approve of me does she?

GBS

You have been very generous towards her.

CHARLOTTE

Only because of you.

GBS

My friends will tell you that I am a bad son, never that she is a bad mother, or rather, no mother. That is why I wish I were an orphan. Now I must get on with my work.

CHARLOTTE

I have decided to go up to London with you next week and see to the house. Then Beatrice and Sydney are coming for a week. Let me take those papers for you. I will type them up in the morning. I'm going to bed. *(Exit)*.

GBS

Dear Ellen,

I have been working 16 hours a day. I have read "YOU NEVER CAN TELL" to the Haymarket Company today. Two hours and forty minutes of it - it's too long. I shall have to spoil it to suit the fashionable dinner hour. Don't go to the Lyceum Theatre tonight! Stay at home and write to me. What does a first night matter? What is their silly curiosity to my heart's need? You may chop off all my fingers and toes for a necklace and have my heart as a locket if you will only say that you like them better than diamonds. I am writing a play for Mrs Patrick Campbell. She has not had a good play for years. She has invited me to tea next week. I hear she has a fierce temper. I am used to actresses and their rages. It will be nothing new.

CHARLOTTE

I've just read this scathing review you wrote of Henry Irving. Why did you do something so stupid? You want Irving to do your play. For two years you have wanted him to produce it! You got Ellen Terry to ask him to do it - then the very day you were to meet with him at the theatre to finalize the production you let your review of his latest production be published in the newspaper. You tore him to shreds. Two columns of it. How could you expect him to accept your play? What were you thinking of?

GBS

Irving has already paid me fifty pounds as an advance for the play.

CHARLOTTE

You think he gave you fifty pounds to do your play. Rubbish! He gave you fifty pounds to shut you up. It is a bribe, don't you see, you silly ass, to keep you from writing reviews of his performance. He will never do your play. Irving is the greatest actor on the British stage. You are a struggling playwright. You want your plays produced, you want Ellen Terry to play in them. What use is it to turn Ellen against Irving and Irving against you? What chance do we have if you alienate all the main players in the theatre? You are a fool to fight against the fact that he is more celebrated than you. Ellen is his leading lady; she works with him every day, every night; she knows the man through and through. Can you imagine how she feels? She believes in you and yet you constantly keep preaching to her that she is being 'used'. No doubt you would use her too if she was available to act in one of your plays. Heaven forbid that she would leave Irving and work for you.

GBS

And, indeed, she never did, but our correspondence continued intermittently for the rest of her life although we hardly ever met.

Enter Ellen Terry

ELLEN

Why, here's a letter from GBS. And he is a vegetarian, is he going too far? I knew of his Jaegerish woolerish ways, but not of the carrots and beans. *(Pause)*. Oh, you perfectly charming being. You are just a duck! Your letter here for supper with my cold chicken pie, and I have not left off laughing all the while. I'm all tired out with caring and caring, and I never leave off, (which is so absurd). But I must hear your plays. Mayn't I have "CANDIDA"? (Pause). Well, I won't write today, but shall take it out in thinking and I shall talk to you tonight when I come home from the theatre and have a quiet time with you. Won't you send me "CANDIDA" one day next week? I'm dull and sick, very, and want an entertainment. Send it to me, like a good boy, as a reward for not letting you hear from me until the end of the week. Your Ellen is very ill, and perhaps may not be fit to act tonight. She probably will, though, for she often acts when she is unfit to stir from her bed. Here's a picture from you! You darling! You knew I would be ill and just want that picture. I'm just going to read your "CANDIDA". I knew you'd send it to me if I were ill. Women get everything if they're sick enough! Truly, at present I'm not fit to get out of bed (where I've been for the last three days) and here am I going to a big stupid dinner tonight. Now for your play. I've cried my poor eyes out over your heavenly play. My dear, and now how can I go out for dinner tonight? I must keep my blue glasses on all the while for my eyes are puffed up and burning. But I can scarce keep from reading it all over again. Oh dear me, I love you more every minute.

I can't help it, and I guessed it would be like that! And so we won't meet. But write more plays, my dear, and let me read them. It has touched me more than I could tell of.

GBS

And then there was the time when I went to the Lyceum Theatre as a critic and Ellen sneaked a look at me through the peephole in the curtain.

ELLEN

I've seen you at last! You ARE a boy! And a duck! But understanding concern. How deadly delicate you look.

GBS

And on the very day that Charlotte and I were married ...

ELLEN

How splendid! What intrepidity to make such a courageous bid for happiness. Into it you both go! Eyes wide open! An example to the world, and may all the gods have you in their keeping.

GBS

No wonder it was said that, in the last quarter of the 19th century, the mark of a young man growing up was when he began to be in love with Ellen Terry. In her later years our meetings were few, and all accidental. One of these chance meetings was on a summer day in the country, near Elstree, where I came upon a crowd of people at work on a cinema film. Ellen was there, acting the heroine. She was astonishingly beautiful. She had passed through that middle phase, so trying to handsome women of matronly amplitude, and was again tall and slender, with a new delicacy and intensity in her saddened expression. She asked me why I did not give her some work in the theatre. "I do not expect leading parts" she said. "I am too old. I am quite willing to play a charwoman." "What would become of the play?! I said. "Imagine a scene in which the part of a canal barge was played by a battleship! What would happen to my play, or to anyone else's, if whenever the charwoman appeared the audience forgot the hero and heroine, and could think of nothing but the wonderful things the charwoman was going to say and do?" It was unanswerable; and we both, I think, felt rather inclined to cry. She became a legend in her old age; but of that I have nothing to say, for we did not meet, and, except for a few broken letters, did not write; and she never was old to me.

Then there was Stella. Stella Patrick Campbell. I went to read her my play "PYGMALION".

MRS CAMPBELL

Dear Mr. Shaw,

What a play. I must confess I was surprised to hear those unpleasant sounds of Eliza's cockney accent coming out of your mouth. But if you're really in earnest the next step is to tell me what the business proposal is - when, where and with whom.

GBS

You knew it would happen! I went calmly to your home to discuss business with you, as hard as nails, and as I am a living man, I fell head over heels in love with you in the first thirty seconds. I dreamed and walked on air all the following afternoon just as if my next birthday was my twentieth.

MRS CAMPBELL

Beatrice Webb is right. You are a sprite, and how can one fall in love with a sprite? Will you come on Friday and I promise we can be alone.

GBS

I am going to break the shattering news that you have captured me ... you must play Eliza. You are an established star, a veteran in fact. I must have an established star. Our friends are beginning to talk about us. I wish I could fall in love without telling everybody. I shall be 56 on the 26th of this month and I have not yet grown up. I must go now and read this letter to my wife, Charlotte. My love affairs are her unfailing amusement.

MRS CAMPBELL

You don't deserve to be as clever as you are and it's not that you are so clever -it's just your exuberant and mischievous mind. I cannot keep up the exuberance like you (*and the beloved Irish accent*). Do something quickly or I shall have vanished. I miss you dreadfully.

GBS

Nearer my goddess by another one hundred and twenty miles. I have never, strangely enough, been here in Orleans before. I should like to do a Joan of Arc play some day. One of my scenes will be Voltaire and Shakespeare running down side streets to avoid meeting her. Would you like to play the maid? You would come in on horseback in shining armor and fight innumerable supers!

MRS CAMPBELL

Your letters are a carnival of words. How can I answer with my poor whining beggars? It will be dreadful when you realize the commonplace, witless charwoman I really am, and you with so many "great women" about you now, Saint Joan and all. I hear you have been ill. Tree at rehearsal suggested giving you a juicy beefsteak for lunch. I told him "for God's sake, no, he's bad enough as it is. If you give him meat, no woman in London will be safe".

It's too late to do anything but accept you and love you - but when you were quite a little boy, somebody ought to have said "hush" just once. I haven't said "kiss me" because life is too short for the kiss my heart calls for look into my but eyes for two minutes without speaking if you dare! Then how many hours would you be late for dinner! Ask Charlotte to be kind. Even if she does think me a lunatic or an adventuress, she might let you call on me when I am ill.

GBS

No. It is best to ask Charlotte nothing. I barely mention your name. Yesterday, a tragedy occurred. She overheard pur telephone conversation and the effect was dreadful. I must, it seems, murder myself, or else murder her. Well, I dare say, it is good for all of us to suffer. I throw my desperate hands to heaven and ask why cannot one make one beloved woman happy without making another miserable

MRS CAMPBELL

I had a dream about Charlotte last night, she shook hands with me warmly and smiled and said "I thought you were a bird of paradise but you were only a silly goose." The dream ended with my jumping out of bed and taking a taxi to your house Stella, la dangereuse. I had an accident while you were away - a bad crash in a taxi, but I am all right now. Visitors by the score - all the people I knew in London. One came every day bringing roses and gaiety in my room. George Cornwallis-West. I think I love him.

GBS

Can it be true? My spirit tells me you are jilting me! Am I spurned indeed? Must I stop making verses? Though I confess I can think of no rhyme for "Stella" but "umbrella" and "too damn well". I love "Mrs. Campbell" and horrors of that sort. Although I like Cornwallis-West I say he is young and I am old. So let him wait until I am tired of you.

MRS CAMPBELL

Be calm, dearest Joey, be gentle with fools. Poor you. Awful as it is, it is nothing compared to the humiliation I feel with Charlotte, while I am without a husband. So please, enough of that. I have just heard of the illness of your beloved mother. I remember you once said "It is from her I derive my brains and character, which does her credit. "Oh Joey! I know how devotedly you love her. If she leaves us, it will be a great loss.

GBS

Mama, yes! She cut a wisdom tooth when she was eighty! And now the end, they say the world is changing horribly.

MRS CAMPBELL

I have just been told the sad news. May she rest in peace! I had a mother who loved Dante and whose soul was steeped in beauty. When you can, let me hear from you. "PYGMALION" went like a dream; it was filled with heavenly laughter. Surely no first night in the world has ever gone so joyously.

GBS

A celebration had been arranged for after the opening. But when I went to fetch Stella I was in for a shock. She had a knack for dramatic timing. I found her on the point of leaving the stage door.

MRS CAMPBELL

Joey ...

GBS

Aren't you going to the party? You're not going home, alone, tonight?

MRS CAMPBELL

I'm not going alone. I'm going home with George. He's waiting for me in his motor car.

GBS

George?

MRS CAMPBELL

Yes, George Cornwallis-West. I married him last Wednesday.

Both exit

Enter Beatrice Webb and Charlotte. Beatrice is packing.

CHARLOTTE

I hope you don't mind my dropping in on you Mrs. Webb.

BEATRICE

It is so good of you to come to visit, but we are packing. Sydney and I are moving to Dorset permanently. I won't see you both for some time. Unless you come and visit.

CHARLOTTE

I would have to come alone, I'm afraid. GBS is too busy to leave right now.

BEATRICE

What do you do now? Now that GBS has two secretaries in London.

CHARLOTTE

And Mrs. Campbell. I am writing a book about myself, believe it or not. It has been difficult but I have come through a bad time and believed GBS was a Bluebeard in disguise. If I'd had a marriage like yours, life would have been very different. Every time I stayed with you I was conscious of the great happiness which was like a radiance in your life together. You had achieved something which I had thought impossible. Could it not happen again? I know perfectly well that my own intellectual capacity was far below his, and this is where our marriage differed from yours. The two of you are so well matched in mind. Still, I have some talents and capacity to use in service for some worthwhile cause.

BEATRICE

So you have finally resigned yourself to his ways.

CHARLOTTE

I was only ever jealous of Stella Campbell. Much of his philandering filled him with shame and disgust, but it did not cure him. It came easily and naturally to him, as to many Irishmen, and it readily and irresistibly appealed to English women unaccustomed to Irish blarney. He tells us - me - how surprised he was when English women took his flatteries and courtesies and endearments for serious intentions instead of light hearted attentions. Often, he had to hastily reverse his engines. However, he learned to put his philandering to severely practical uses and to employ it as a means for obtaining, first the interest, then the goodwill, and finally the co-operation and services of famous actresses. He succeeded. What he was trying to do was both human and natural. He'd spent nine years writing. Nine years of poverty in London with no success . So it does show clearly that if he was both saint and sage in some respects, he was a practical person with an eye to the main chance. He succeeded. Come on, let's go for a walk.

GBS

I grow old apace -1 have lost all differentiated interest in women and am bored by their redoubled interest in me. Probably, I ought to die. Since Charlotte's death I have had some offers of marriage and since having only a few years -quite probably a few days - to live, my widow would be well provided for. But I have had enough of marriage and I am quite happy alone. I inherit from my mother a great capacity for solitude in my own company. Marriage is an acquired taste, like olives or eating winkles with a pin. Perhaps I ought never to have been married.

I realize now that some of my most gratifying relationships with women were on paper. Well, let those who may complain that it was all on paper. Remember that only on paper has humanity yet achieved truth, beauty, virtue, and abiding love.

Goodbye, goodbye, goodbye.

Barry Morse

Ellen Terry

Charlotte Payne Townshend

In praise of 'Passionate Pilgrimages..from Chopin to Coward. Published by Welcome Rain Publishers, NYC.

"Elizabeth Sharland will squire you to places you never thought you'd go, in impeccable language and with rare grace. Learn, then, how George Sand whiled away the hours with Chopin at Chateau de Nohant, and spend some time with Somerset Maugham at Cap Ferrat near Nice. Katherine Mansfield charms us in Menton, alongside Franco Zeffirelli in Positano, Italy, Cole Porter in Paris, Paul Bowles in Morocco and Lady Gregory in Ireland. The illustrations are lavish, offering visual clues to the geniuses that inhabit these pages. Travel with Sharland as you have never travelled before ...a blessing on your cranium."

- Malachy McCourt (Irish-American actor/writer)

"BEYOND THE DOORS OF NOTORIOUS COVENT GARDEN"
REVIEWED by Scott Eyman, Palm Beach Post, Palm Beach Florida.

Love London? Guide to Covent Garden just for you

By Scott Eyman
Palm Beach Post Books Editor

I have a friend who's a devout Anglophile, traveling to London every year to see some shows and, mostly, walk around town and bask. He will, I suspect, love Elizabeth Sharland's Behind the Doors of Covent Garden, a book that covers the years from Bonnie Prince Charlie and Nell Gwynn to Princess Diana.

There's a particularly interesting chapter here on the theaters of Covent Garden, among them the magnificent Drury Lane, which has housed everything from the great Ivor Novello shows of the 1930s to Miss Saigon, which ran for at least a decade. The book also includes a lovely guide to interesting shops in the area, including Pleasures of Past Times in Cecil Court, my favorite London bookshop — actually, my favorite bookshop in the world.

Sharland, who spends part of the year in Palm Beach, knows every foot of the place — I didn't know that the Palm Court of the Waldorf

Hotel was modeled after the Palm Court of the Titanic! — and does justice to it in her rich and spirited book.

Further books by Elizabeth Sharland are available on Amazon.com Barnes and Nobles.com and Amazon.co.uk www.sharland.com

About the Author

ELIZABETH SHARLAND is an actress, producer, playwright and novelist, best-known for her informative and entertaining non-fiction books about theatre stars - and for her popular and long-running show Love From Shakespeare to Coward, an anthology of plays poems, letters and diaries around the theme of love, based on six years in the West End using over 200 actors in showcases.

Recently she performed at the Bruno Auditorium at the Lincoln Center presenting her new book, "Behind the Doors of Notorious Covent Garden." With Steve Ross and Tammy Grimes. Elizabeth is the Food and Entertainment Editor of the Palm Beach Society Magazine, reviewing restaurants and theatres in Palm Beach, Florida. She trained at the Guildhall School of Music and Drama and joined the Old Vic Company to tour Australia. She has had plays produced in London and New York, formed an English-speaking theatre company in Paris, worked for Yul Brynner on Broadway, and also lectures regularly on the Queen Mary 2, between London and New York. She is married to a Dublin-born psychiatrist, has one son, and travels frequently between Europe and America.